EMMANUEL JOSEPH

Speak, Lead, Act, The Trifecta of Public Speaking, Leadership, and Bold Decision-Making

Copyright © 2025 by Emmanuel Joseph

All rights reserved. No part of this publication may be reproduced, stored or transmitted in any form or by any means, electronic, mechanical, photocopying, recording, scanning, or otherwise without written permission from the publisher. It is illegal to copy this book, post it to a website, or distribute it by any other means without permission.

First edition

This book was professionally typeset on Reedsy.
Find out more at reedsy.com

Contents

1	Chapter 1: The Power of Words	1
2	Chapter 2: Finding Your Voice	3
3	Chapter 3: Engaging Your Audience	5
4	Chapter 4: The Art of Persuasion	7
5	Chapter 5: Overcoming Fear and Anxiety	9
6	Chapter 6: Crafting a Compelling Message	11
7	Chapter 7: Mastering Non-Verbal Communication	13
8	Chapter 8: Building Rapport with Your Audience	15
9	Chapter 9: Handling Difficult Questions and Situations	17
10	Chapter 10: Leveraging Technology in Public Speaking	19
11	Chapter 11: Cultivating Emotional Intelligence	21
12	Chapter 12: The Role of Ethics in Public Speaking	23
13	Chapter 13: Developing a Personal Leadership Style	25
14	Chapter 14: Making Bold Decisions	27
15	Chapter 15: Building and Leading High-Performing Teams	28
16	Chapter 16: Leading Through Change	30
17	Chapter 17: Leading with Vision	31

1

Chapter 1: The Power of Words

In the world of public speaking, words are your most valuable asset. They have the power to inspire, motivate, and influence people in ways that few other tools can. From famous speeches that have moved nations to personal anecdotes that touch hearts, the right words can make all the difference. A well-chosen phrase can evoke emotion, spark action, and even change the course of history. The ability to harness this power begins with understanding the importance of words and their impact.

When speaking to an audience, consider the weight of your words. Reflect on the messages that have left a lasting impression on you and dissect what made them powerful. Was it the eloquence of the speaker, the relatability of the story, or the clarity of the message? By identifying these elements, you can begin to craft speeches that resonate deeply with your audience. Use metaphors, analogies, and vivid imagery to paint a picture with your words, making your message more memorable and impactful.

Moreover, the power of words is not just about what you say, but how you say it. Tone, pacing, and emphasis play a significant role in conveying your message effectively. A well-timed pause can add dramatic effect, while varying your tone can keep the audience engaged. Practice and refine your delivery to ensure that your words are not only heard but felt. Rehearsing in front of a mirror or recording yourself can help you identify areas for improvement and build your confidence.

In the chapters to come, we will explore various techniques to enhance your public speaking skills, but always remember: at the heart of great public speaking lies the power of words. They are the building blocks of your message, and when used wisely, they can inspire and lead others towards positive change. Whether you're addressing a small group or a large audience, the right words delivered with passion and conviction can leave a lasting impression and drive meaningful action.

2

Chapter 2: Finding Your Voice

Your voice is unique, and it's crucial to find and embrace it in public speaking. This chapter will guide you through the process of discovering your authentic voice, building confidence, and projecting your message clearly and compellingly. The first step in finding your voice is understanding your strengths and weaknesses. Take time to reflect on your personal experiences, values, and beliefs. These elements shape your perspective and can add depth to your speeches.

Building confidence is a key aspect of finding your voice. Confidence comes from preparation and practice. The more you practice, the more comfortable you will become with your material and delivery. Start by practicing in front of a mirror, then gradually move to small groups of friends or family. Seek constructive feedback and use it to improve. Remember, even the most seasoned speakers experience nervousness; it's how you channel that energy that makes the difference.

Projecting your message clearly and compellingly requires attention to both verbal and non-verbal communication. Your body language, facial expressions, and gestures all play a role in how your message is received. Stand tall, make eye contact, and use open gestures to convey confidence and sincerity. Vary your tone, pace, and volume to keep your audience engaged. Pay attention to the rhythm of your speech; a well-placed pause can emphasize important points and give your audience time to absorb your message.

Finding your voice is an ongoing journey. As you gain more experience and receive feedback, your voice will continue to evolve. Stay true to yourself and your message, and don't be afraid to let your personality shine through. Authenticity is key to connecting with your audience. When you speak from the heart, your message becomes more relatable and impactful. Remember, the goal is not to be perfect but to be genuine and persuasive.

3

Chapter 3: Engaging Your Audience

Engagement is the key to successful public speaking. In this chapter, we'll explore techniques for capturing and maintaining your audience's attention. One of the most effective ways to engage your audience is through storytelling. Stories have the power to captivate and resonate on an emotional level. Start with a compelling narrative that relates to your message. Use descriptive language and vivid imagery to draw your audience into the story. A well-told story can make your message more relatable and memorable.

Humor is another powerful tool for engaging your audience. When used appropriately, humor can lighten the mood and create a bond with your listeners. It can also make your message more approachable and enjoyable. However, be mindful of your audience's sensibilities and avoid humor that may be offensive or inappropriate. A light-hearted joke or an amusing anecdote can go a long way in keeping your audience engaged and entertained.

Relatability is crucial for connecting with your audience. Put yourself in their shoes and consider their needs, interests, and concerns. Tailor your message to address these factors and make it relevant to their lives. Use inclusive language and examples that your audience can relate to. Engage them with questions, polls, or interactive activities. Encourage participation and feedback to create a dynamic and interactive speaking experience. The more your audience feels involved, the more engaged they will be.

Reading the room and adapting your message is essential for maintaining engagement. Pay attention to your audience's reactions and adjust your delivery accordingly. If you notice that they're losing interest, inject energy into your speech with a change of pace or a surprising fact. Be flexible and willing to deviate from your script if needed. Respond to feedback and address any questions or concerns that arise. By being attuned to your audience, you can create a meaningful connection and leave a lasting impact.

4

Chapter 4: The Art of Persuasion

Persuasion is a powerful tool in public speaking. It allows you to influence your audience's thoughts, beliefs, and actions. In this chapter, we'll delve into the principles of persuasion, such as ethos, pathos, and logos. Ethos refers to the credibility and authority of the speaker, while pathos appeals to the audience's emotions. Logos, on the other hand, relies on logical reasoning and evidence. Understanding these principles can help you build a strong foundation for your persuasive efforts.

We'll explore techniques for building credibility, appealing to emotions, and presenting logical arguments. To build credibility, it's important to establish your expertise and trustworthiness. Share your qualifications, experiences, and relevant knowledge with your audience. Be honest and transparent in your communication, and always strive to uphold your integrity. By building trust with your audience, you'll be more effective in persuading them to adopt your viewpoint.

Appealing to emotions involves connecting with your audience on a personal level. Use storytelling, vivid imagery, and relatable examples to evoke emotions such as empathy, excitement, or concern. Emotional appeals can create a strong bond between you and your audience, making your message more impactful. However, it's important to balance emotional appeals with logical reasoning to ensure that your arguments are well-rounded and credible.

Presenting logical arguments requires careful organization and clarity. Structure your speech in a way that logically progresses from one point to the next. Use evidence, statistics, and examples to support your claims. Address counterarguments and provide thoughtful rebuttals to demonstrate your thorough understanding of the topic. By combining ethos, pathos, and logos, you'll be able to create persuasive speeches that resonate with your audience and drive them to take action.

5

Chapter 5: Overcoming Fear and Anxiety

Public speaking can be a daunting task, even for seasoned speakers. Fear and anxiety are common challenges that can hinder your ability to communicate effectively. In this chapter, we'll explore strategies for overcoming these challenges and building confidence in your speaking abilities. Recognize that it's normal to feel nervous before speaking, and that many great speakers have faced similar challenges.

One effective strategy for managing anxiety is preparation. The more prepared you are, the more confident you'll feel. Research your topic thoroughly, organize your speech, and practice delivering it multiple times. Familiarize yourself with the venue and visualize yourself speaking confidently in front of your audience. Visualization can help reduce anxiety by mentally rehearsing success.

Deep breathing exercises can also help calm your nerves. Take slow, deep breaths before and during your speech to relax your body and mind. Practice mindfulness techniques to stay present in the moment and avoid getting overwhelmed by negative thoughts. Positive self-talk can also boost your confidence. Replace self-doubt with affirmations such as "I am prepared and capable" or "I can handle this."

Building confidence takes time and experience. Start by speaking in front of small, supportive groups and gradually increase the size of your audience. Seek constructive feedback and use it to improve your skills. Remember that nervousness is a natural part of public speaking, and that with practice, you can learn to manage it effectively. By facing your fears and developing your confidence, you'll become a more effective and compelling speaker.

6

Chapter 6: Crafting a Compelling Message

A compelling message is at the heart of effective public speaking. In this chapter, we'll explore the elements of crafting a message that resonates with your audience. Start by identifying your core message or main point. What do you want your audience to take away from your speech? Having a clear and focused message will help you structure your speech and ensure that your audience understands your key points.

Once you've identified your core message, think about how to present it in a way that captures your audience's attention. Use a strong opening to grab their interest and set the tone for your speech. This could be a surprising fact, a thought-provoking question, or a powerful quote. Follow up with a well-organized body that logically progresses from one point to the next. Use transitions to guide your audience through your speech and reinforce your key points.

To make your message more engaging, use storytelling, anecdotes, and examples. Stories have the power to connect with your audience on an emotional level and make your message more memorable. Choose stories that are relevant to your message and illustrate your points effectively. Use descriptive language and vivid imagery to bring your stories to life.

Finally, end with a strong conclusion that reinforces your core message and leaves a lasting impression. Summarize your key points and provide a call to action, encouraging your audience to take the next step. A well-crafted message, delivered with passion and clarity, can inspire and motivate your audience to take action and make a difference.

7

Chapter 7: Mastering Non-Verbal Communication

Non-verbal communication plays a crucial role in public speaking. Your body language, facial expressions, and gestures can significantly impact how your message is received. In this chapter, we'll explore the importance of non-verbal communication and how to use it effectively. Start by being aware of your body language. Stand tall and maintain good posture to convey confidence and authority. Avoid crossing your arms or fidgeting, as these behaviors can be distracting and make you appear nervous.

Facial expressions are another important aspect of non-verbal communication. Smile to create a friendly and approachable demeanor. Use your facial expressions to convey emotions and emphasize your message. For example, raise your eyebrows to show surprise or nod your head to indicate agreement. Make eye contact with your audience to build a connection and demonstrate sincerity. Avoid looking down or scanning the room too quickly, as this can make you appear disengaged.

Gestures can also enhance your message and make your speech more dynamic. Use hand gestures to emphasize key points and add visual interest to your presentation. Be mindful of your gestures and avoid overdoing them, as excessive gesturing can be distracting. Practice your gestures to ensure they appear natural and purposeful. Remember that non-verbal communication should complement your verbal message, not overshadow it.

Incorporating non-verbal communication into your public speaking can enhance your delivery and make your message more impactful. By being aware of your body language, facial expressions, and gestures, you can create a more engaging and persuasive presentation. Practice and refine your non-verbal communication skills to ensure that you are effectively conveying your message to your audience.

8

Chapter 8: Building Rapport with Your Audience

Building rapport with your audience is essential for successful public speaking. When your audience feels connected to you, they are more likely to be engaged and receptive to your message. In this chapter, we'll explore strategies for building rapport and establishing a positive relationship with your audience. Start by being genuine and authentic. People are more likely to trust and connect with you if they believe you are being sincere. Share personal anecdotes and experiences to create a sense of relatability and trust.

Active listening is another important aspect of building rapport. Show your audience that you value their input and feedback. Encourage participation and respond thoughtfully to questions and comments. Use inclusive language and address your audience directly to create a sense of connection. Make an effort to remember and use people's names when addressing them.

Empathy is also crucial for building rapport. Put yourself in your audience's shoes and consider their needs, interests, and concerns. Show understanding and compassion for their experiences and perspectives. By demonstrating empathy, you can create a more positive and supportive environment that fosters engagement and connection.

Building rapport takes time and effort, but it is essential for effective public speaking. By being genuine, actively listening, and showing empathy, you can create a strong connection with your audience. This connection will make your message more impactful and increase the likelihood of achieving your desired outcomes.

9

Chapter 9: Handling Difficult Questions and Situations

In public speaking, you may encounter difficult questions or challenging situations. Handling these moments with grace and confidence is essential for maintaining your credibility and rapport with your audience. In this chapter, we'll explore strategies for addressing difficult questions and managing challenging situations. Start by staying calm and composed. Take a deep breath and give yourself a moment to think before responding. Remaining calm will help you stay focused and communicate more effectively.

When addressing difficult questions, it's important to listen carefully and fully understand the question before responding. Paraphrase the question to ensure you have understood it correctly and to buy yourself some time to formulate your response. Be honest and transparent in your answers. If you don't know the answer, it's okay to admit it. Offer to follow up with more information later if possible.

In challenging situations, it's important to stay respectful and professional. Avoid getting defensive or argumentative. Instead, acknowledge the concern or issue raised and address it thoughtfully. Use empathy and understanding to de-escalate tense situations and find common ground. If necessary, redirect the conversation back to your main points and maintain control of the discussion.

By staying calm, listening carefully, and responding thoughtfully, you can handle difficult questions and situations with confidence. These skills will help you maintain your credibility and rapport with your audience, even in challenging moments. Practice these strategies to ensure you are prepared for any situation that may arise during your public speaking engagements.

10

Chapter 10: Leveraging Technology in Public Speaking

In today's digital age, technology plays a significant role in public speaking. From presentation software to virtual meetings, leveraging technology can enhance your delivery and engagement with your audience. In this chapter, we'll explore various tools and techniques for incorporating technology into your public speaking. Start by familiarizing yourself with popular presentation software such as PowerPoint or Keynote. These tools allow you to create visually appealing slides that complement your message and keep your audience engaged.

Virtual meetings and webinars have become increasingly common, especially in the wake of the COVID-19 pandemic. Understanding how to navigate these platforms and effectively communicate in a virtual setting is essential. Invest in quality audio and video equipment to ensure clear communication. Practice using the platform's features, such as screen sharing and chat functions, to enhance your presentation. Remember to maintain eye contact with the camera to create a sense of connection with your virtual audience.

Interactive technology can also enhance audience engagement. Consider using polling tools, live Q&A sessions, or interactive whiteboards to encourage participation and gather feedback. These tools can make your presentation more dynamic and interactive, keeping your audience involved and attentive. Be mindful of technical difficulties and have a backup plan in place to address any issues that may arise.

By leveraging technology, you can enhance your public speaking and create a more engaging and impactful presentation. Stay updated with the latest tools and trends to continually improve your skills and adapt to the evolving landscape of public speaking. Technology can be a powerful ally in delivering your message effectively and connecting with your audience.

11

Chapter 11: Cultivating Emotional Intelligence

Emotional intelligence (EI) is the ability to understand and manage your own emotions, as well as the emotions of others. In public speaking, EI is crucial for building rapport, engaging your audience, and delivering your message effectively. In this chapter, we'll explore the components of emotional intelligence and how to cultivate them. Start by developing self-awareness. Reflect on your emotions, strengths, and weaknesses. Understand how your emotions impact your communication and interactions with others.

Self-regulation is another important aspect of EI. Learn to manage your emotions and respond to challenging situations calmly and thoughtfully. Practice mindfulness techniques to stay present and focused during your speeches. Develop strategies for handling stress and anxiety, such as deep breathing exercises or visualization. By managing your emotions effectively, you can maintain composure and deliver your message confidently.

Empathy is a key component of emotional intelligence. Put yourself in your audience's shoes and consider their perspectives and feelings. Show understanding and compassion for their experiences and concerns. Use your empathetic insights to tailor your message and connect with your audience on a deeper level. Active listening and genuine engagement with your audience can also enhance your empathetic abilities.

Social skills are essential for building relationships and engaging your audience. Practice effective communication techniques, such as active listening, clear articulation, and open body language. Build strong relationships with your audience by being approachable, respectful, and responsive. By cultivating emotional intelligence, you can enhance your public speaking skills and create a more positive and impactful experience for your audience.

12

Chapter 12: The Role of Ethics in Public Speaking

Ethics play a crucial role in public speaking. As a speaker, you have a responsibility to communicate truthfully, respectfully, and responsibly. In this chapter, we'll explore the principles of ethical public speaking and how to uphold them. Start by being honest and transparent in your communication. Present accurate information and avoid misleading or deceptive practices. Cite your sources and give credit to others' work to maintain integrity.

Respect for your audience is another important aspect of ethical public speaking. Consider the diversity of your audience and be mindful of cultural, social, and individual differences. Avoid offensive or discriminatory language and behavior. Show respect for differing viewpoints and engage in constructive dialogue. By fostering an inclusive and respectful environment, you can build trust and credibility with your audience.

Responsibility involves considering the potential impact of your message. Reflect on the consequences of your words and actions. Avoid spreading misinformation or promoting harmful behaviors. Use your platform to promote positive change and contribute to the well-being of your audience. Be accountable for your communication and be willing to address any mistakes or misunderstandings that may arise.

By upholding ethical principles, you can build trust, credibility, and respect with your audience. Ethical public speaking not only enhances your reputation but also contributes to a more positive and constructive discourse. Practice ethical communication in all your public speaking engagements to create a more meaningful and impactful experience for your audience.

13

Chapter 13: Developing a Personal Leadership Style

Leadership is a unique and personal journey. In this chapter, we'll explore the importance of developing your own leadership style and how it can enhance your effectiveness as a leader. Start by reflecting on your values, beliefs, and experiences. These elements shape your perspective and influence your leadership approach. Consider the leaders you admire and the qualities that make them effective. Use these insights to identify the characteristics and behaviors you want to embody as a leader.

Building self-awareness is crucial for developing your leadership style. Understand your strengths and weaknesses, and seek feedback from others to gain different perspectives. Use this information to develop a growth mindset and continuously improve your skills. Embrace your unique qualities and leverage them to create a leadership style that is authentic and effective.

Adaptability is another important aspect of leadership. Different situations and teams may require different approaches. Be flexible and willing to adjust your style to meet the needs of your team and the circumstances. By being adaptable, you can build stronger relationships and foster a positive and productive work environment.

Developing a personal leadership style takes time and effort, but it is essential for effective leadership. By reflecting on your values, building self-awareness, and embracing adaptability, you can create a leadership approach that is authentic, effective, and impactful.

14

Chapter 14: Making Bold Decisions

Bold decision-making is a key component of effective leadership. In this chapter, we'll explore the principles of making bold decisions and how to apply them in your leadership journey. Start by understanding the importance of taking risks and being willing to step outside your comfort zone. Bold decisions often involve uncertainty and potential challenges, but they can also lead to significant growth and success.

Gathering information and analyzing the situation is crucial for making informed decisions. Take the time to research and understand the context, consider different perspectives, and evaluate the potential risks and benefits. Use critical thinking and problem-solving skills to identify the best course of action.

Trusting your instincts and intuition is also important in bold decision-making. While data and analysis are valuable, sometimes you need to rely on your gut feelings and experiences. Trust yourself and have confidence in your ability to make the right decisions. Communicate your decisions clearly and confidently to your team, and be prepared to take responsibility for the outcomes.

Bold decision-making requires courage, confidence, and a willingness to take risks. By gathering information, trusting your instincts, and communicating effectively, you can make bold decisions that drive success and inspire your team.

15

Chapter 15: Building and Leading High-Performing Teams

Building and leading high-performing teams is essential for achieving organizational success. In this chapter, we'll explore the principles of team building and effective leadership. Start by creating a clear vision and set of goals for your team. Communicate these goals clearly and ensure that each team member understands their role and responsibilities. Establish a culture of collaboration, trust, and accountability.

Recruiting and retaining talented individuals is crucial for building a high-performing team. Look for individuals who possess the skills, knowledge, and values that align with your team's goals. Provide opportunities for professional development and growth to keep your team members engaged and motivated. Recognize and reward their contributions to foster a positive and supportive work environment.

Effective communication is essential for leading a high-performing team. Foster open and transparent communication, encourage feedback, and actively listen to your team members. Address any conflicts or issues promptly and constructively. By maintaining open lines of communication, you can build trust and ensure that everyone is working towards the same goals.

Building and leading high-performing teams requires vision, communication, and a commitment to fostering a positive and supportive work environment. By recruiting talented individuals, providing opportunities for growth, and maintaining open communication, you can create a team that is motivated, engaged, and successful.

16

Chapter 16: Leading Through Change

Change is inevitable in any organization, and effective leaders must be able to navigate and lead through it. In this chapter, we'll explore the principles of leading through change and how to apply them in your leadership journey. Start by understanding the nature of change and its impact on your team. Recognize that change can be challenging and unsettling for many people.

Communicate the reasons for the change clearly and transparently. Help your team understand the benefits and implications of the change, and address any concerns or questions they may have. Provide support and resources to help them adapt to the new situation. Be empathetic and understanding, and acknowledge the emotions and challenges that come with change.

Involve your team in the change process as much as possible. Encourage their input and feedback, and involve them in decision-making. By involving your team, you can build buy-in and commitment to the change. Recognize and celebrate small wins and milestones along the way to maintain morale and motivation.

Leading through change requires clear communication, empathy, and involvement. By understanding the impact of change, communicating effectively, and involving your team, you can navigate change successfully and lead your team through it.

17

Chapter 17: Leading with Vision

Leadership is not just about managing people; it's about inspiring them to achieve great things. In this final chapter, we'll discuss the importance of having a clear vision and the ability to communicate it effectively. A strong vision provides direction and purpose, motivating your team to work towards a common goal. Reflect on your long-term goals and aspirations for your organization or team, and articulate a compelling vision that aligns with these goals.

Communicating your vision effectively is crucial for inspiring and motivating your team. Use storytelling, vivid imagery, and clear language to convey your vision in a way that resonates with your audience. Share your passion and enthusiasm for the vision, and explain how it benefits both the organization and the individuals involved. Regularly reinforce the vision through your actions and communication to keep it top of mind.

Leading with vision also involves setting clear goals and expectations, and providing the support and resources needed to achieve them. Empower your team members to take ownership of their roles and contribute to the vision. Foster a culture of collaboration, innovation, and continuous improvement to drive progress towards the vision.

Leading with vision is the ultimate goal of the trifecta of public speaking, leadership, and bold decision-making. By having a clear vision, communicating it effectively, and empowering your team to achieve it, you can inspire and lead others towards positive change and success.

Speak, Lead, Act: The Trifecta of Public Speaking, Leadership, and Bold Decision-Making

In a world where effective communication and decisive leadership are paramount, "Speak, Lead, Act" serves as a comprehensive guide to mastering these essential skills. This book delves into the art of public speaking, the nuances of leadership, and the courage required for bold decision-making, offering practical insights and strategies for individuals seeking to enhance their influence and impact.

Through seventeen engaging chapters, "Speak, Lead, Act" explores the power of words, the importance of finding your authentic voice, and techniques for engaging and persuading audiences. It addresses common challenges such as overcoming fear and anxiety, crafting compelling messages, and leveraging technology in public speaking. The book also emphasizes the significance of non-verbal communication, emotional intelligence, and ethical considerations in both speaking and leadership.

In addition to public speaking, "Speak, Lead, Act" provides valuable guidance on developing a personal leadership style, building high-performing teams, and navigating change. It underscores the importance of having a clear vision and the ability to communicate it effectively, inspiring readers to lead with purpose and confidence.

Whether you're an aspiring speaker, a seasoned leader, or someone looking to make bold decisions, "Speak, Lead, Act" offers a wealth of knowledge and practical advice to help you succeed. With real-world examples, actionable tips, and insightful reflections, this book empowers you to speak with confidence, lead with vision, and act decisively in any situation.

www.ingramcontent.com/pod-product-compliance
Lightning Source LLC
LaVergne TN
LVHW020500080526
838202LV00057B/6078